PARAMEDICS

PEOPLE WHO KEEP US SAFE

Ruth Daly

LIGHTBOX
openlightbox.com

LIGHTBOX

Go to **www.openlightbox.com** and enter this book's unique code.

ACCESS CODE

LBXE9273

Lightbox is an all-inclusive digital solution for the teaching and learning of curriculum topics in an original, groundbreaking way. Lightbox is based on National Curriculum Standards.

OPTIMIZED FOR

- ✓ **TABLETS**
- ✓ **WHITEBOARDS**
- ✓ **COMPUTERS**
- ✓ **AND MUCH MORE!**

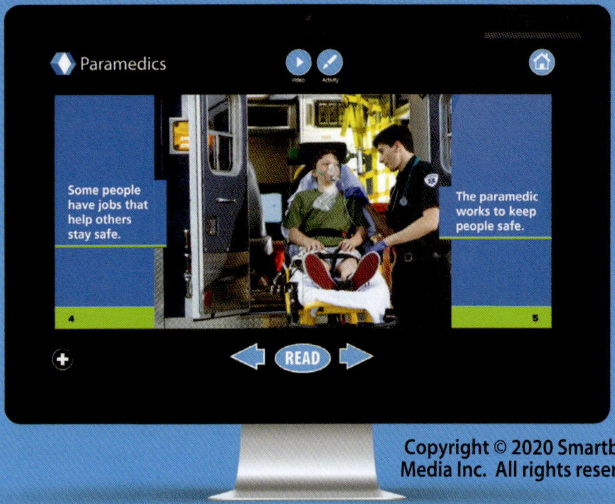

STANDARD FEATURES OF LIGHTBOX

AUDIO High-quality narration using text-to-speech system

VIDEOS Embedded high-definition video clips

ACTIVITIES Printable PDFs that can be emailed and graded

WEBLINKS Curated links to external, child-safe resources

SLIDESHOWS Pictorial overviews of key concepts

INTERACTIVE MAPS Interactive maps and aerial satellite imagery

QUIZZES Ten multiple choice questions that are automatically graded and emailed for teacher assessment

KEY WORDS Matching key concepts to their definitions

VIDEOS

WEBLINKS

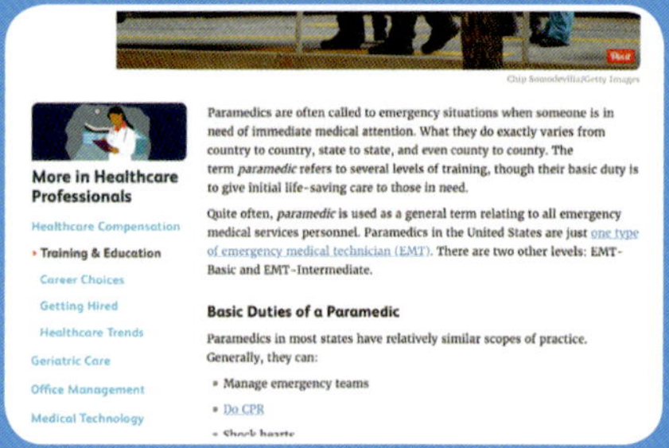

SLIDESHOWS

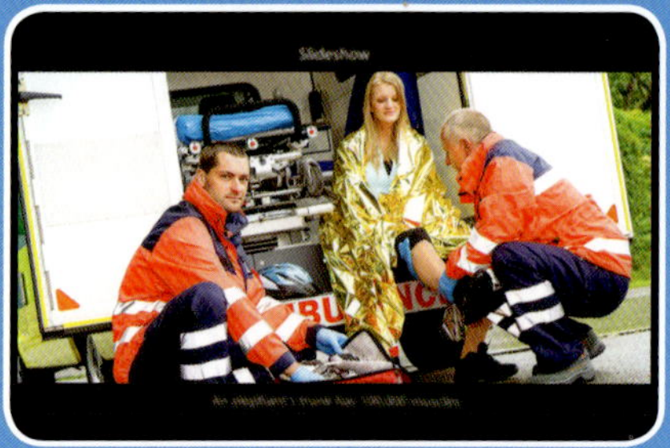

QUIZZES

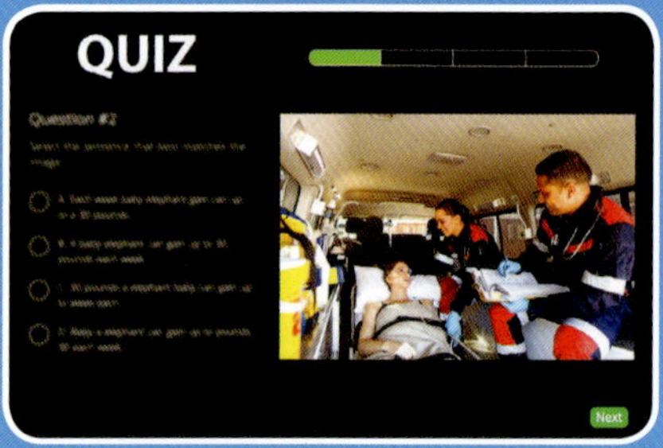

PARAMEDICS

PEOPLE WHO KEEP US SAFE

CONTENTS

Some people have jobs that help others stay safe.

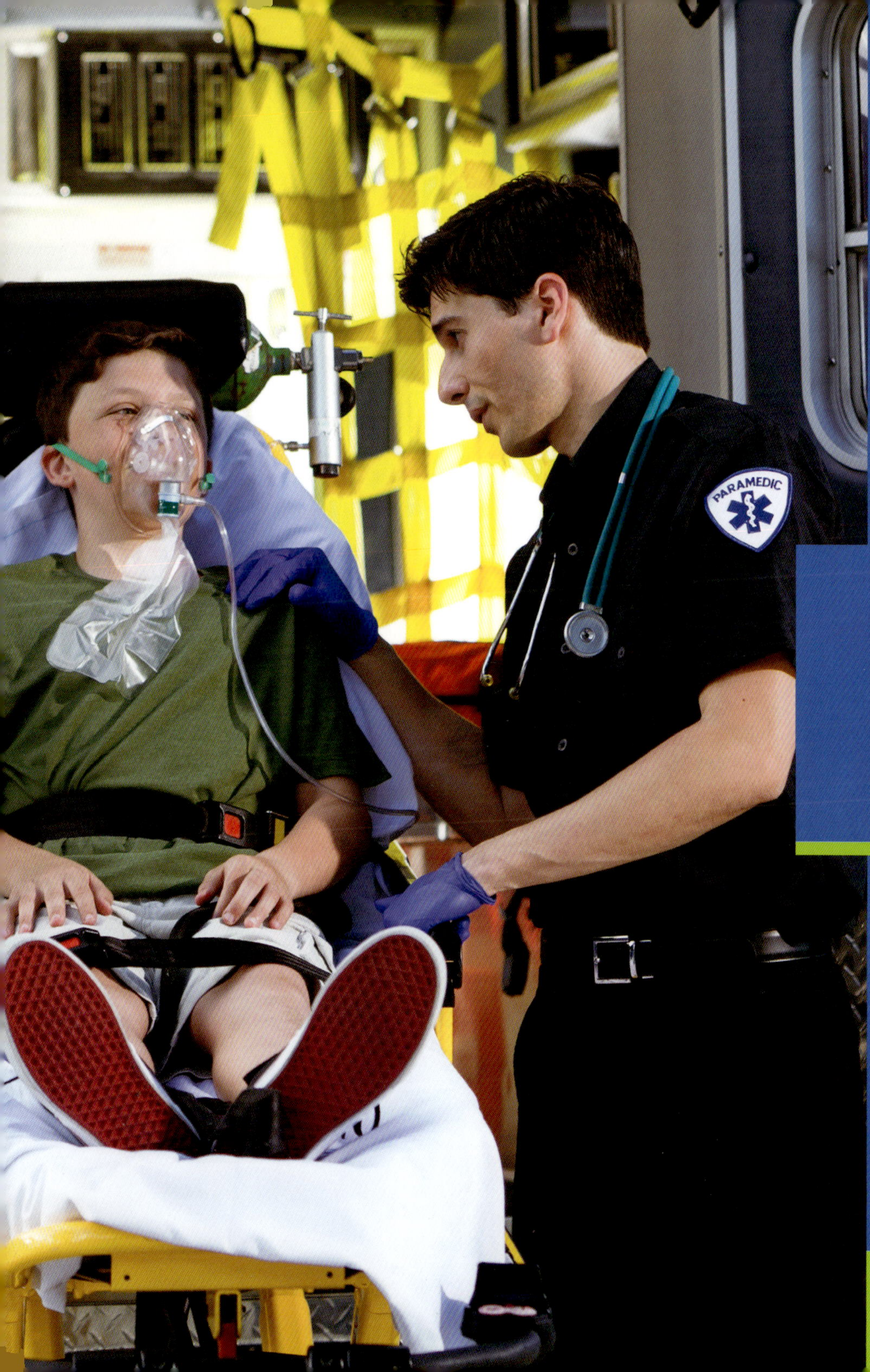

The paramedic works to keep people safe.

A paramedic works in an ambulance.

Ambulances can take people who are badly hurt or very sick to hospitals.

The first hospital ambulance service was created for the Commercial Hospital, in Cincinnati, Ohio.

A paramedic takes care of people before they get to the hospital.

He uses tools inside the ambulance to help them feel better.

The paramedic checks to see where someone is hurt.

There are more than **250,000** paramedics in the United States.

He records what is wrong so he can tell the doctor.

The paramedic uses a special bed to move people from one place to another.

It has legs
that fold up.
This helps
it fit inside
an ambulance
or helicopter.

The paramedic puts a bandage over cuts to keep them clean.

He uses a splint if a bone is broken. The splint keeps the bone still.

Sometimes a paramedic helps people who can not breathe.

He uses a special machine to help them breathe again.

A person **must study for about** 1,200 hours **to become** a paramedic.

A paramedic must keep his ambulance clean at all times.

He also makes sure there are enough supplies for each day.

Paramedics are important because they keep us safe.

See what you have learned about paramedics.

Describe what you see in each of the pictures.

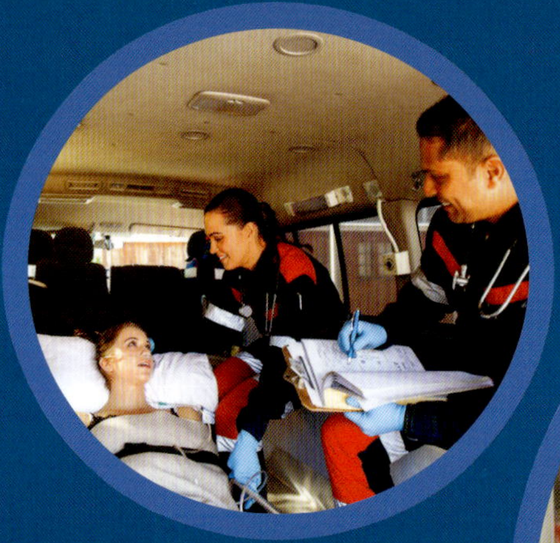

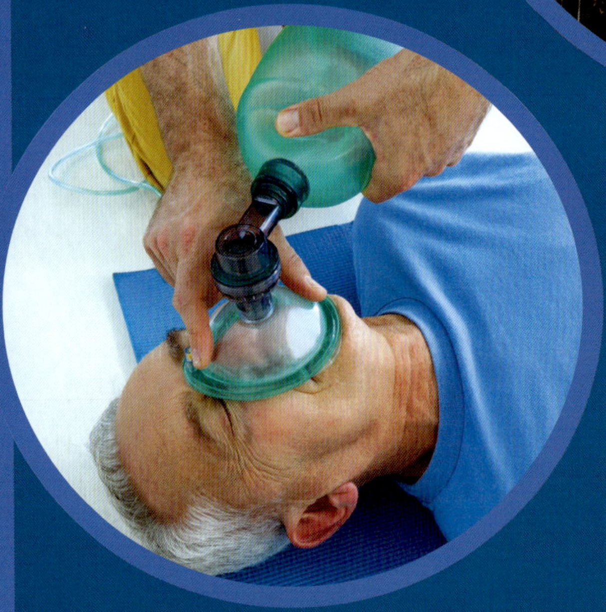

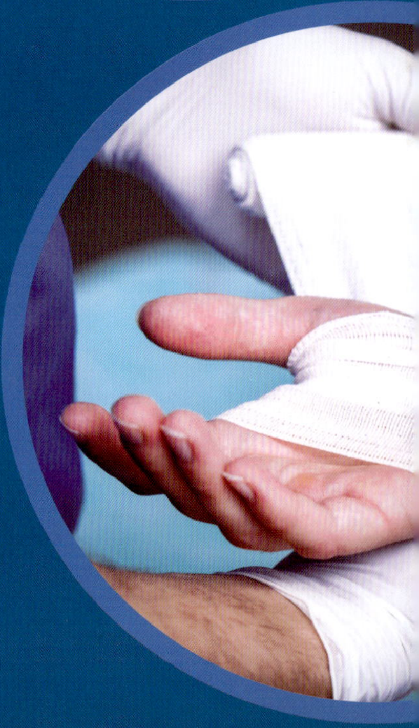

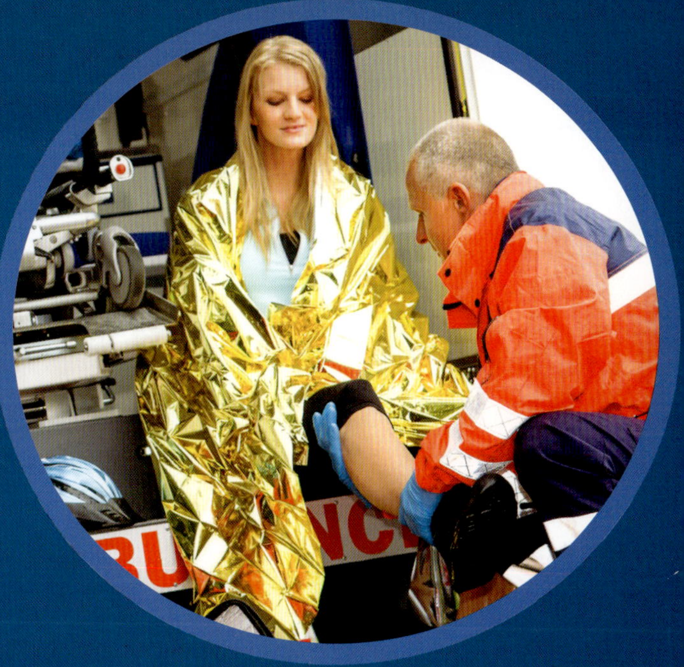

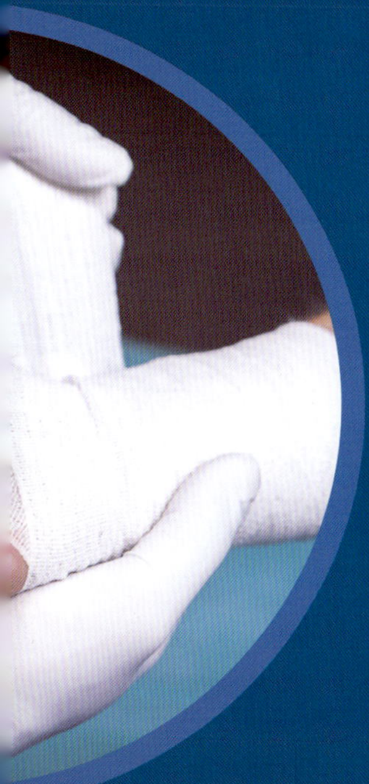

AMBULANCE

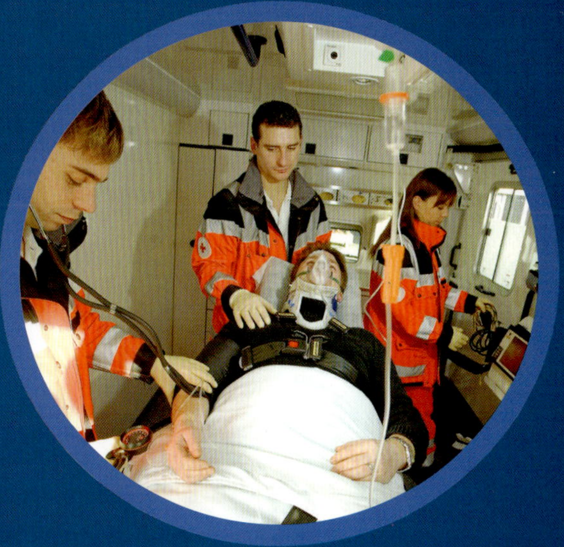

KEY WORDS

Research has shown that as much as 65 percent of all written material published in English is made up of 300 words. These 300 words cannot be taught using pictures or learned by sounding them out. They must be recognized by sight. This book contains 70 common sight words to help young readers improve their reading fluency and comprehension. This book also teaches young readers several important content words, such as proper nouns. These words are paired with pictures to aid in learning and improve understanding.

Page	Sight Words First Appearance
4	have, help, others, people, some, that
5	keep, the, to, works
6	a, an, in
7	are, can, first, for, or, take, very, was, who
8	before, get, of, they
9	he, them, uses
10	is, more, see, states, than, there, where
11	so, tell, what
12	another, from, move, one, place
13	has, it, this, up
14	cuts, over, puts
15	if, still
16	sometimes
17	about, again, must, study
18	all, at, his, times
19	also, day, each, enough, makes
20	because, important, us

Page	Content Words First Appearance
4	jobs
5	paramedic
6	ambulance
7	ambulance service, Cincinnati, Commercial Hospital, hospitals, Ohio
9	tools
10	United States
11	doctor
12	bed
13	helicopter, legs
14	bandage
15	bone, splint
17	hours, machine, person
19	supplies

Published by Smartbook Media Inc.
350 5th Avenue, 59th Floor New York, NY 10118
Website: www.openlightbox.com

Library of Congress Control Number: 2019941560

ISBN 978-1-5105-4599-1 (hardcover)
ISBN 978-1-5105-4600-4 (multi-user eBook)

Printed in Guangzhou, China
1 2 3 4 5 6 7 8 9 0 23 22 21 20 19

052019
122918

Project Coordinator: Sara Cucini
Art Director: Terry Paulhus

Every reasonable effort has been made to trace ownership and to obtain permission to reprint copyright material. The publisher would be pleased to have any errors or omissions brought to its attention so that they may be corrected in subsequent printings.

The publisher acknowledges Alamy, Dreamstime, Getty Images, iStock, and Shutterstock as the primary image suppliers for this title.